TANDEM

Bawdy Barrack-room Ballads

From Stockport to Sevastopol, from Surrey to the Sudan, the British Tommy has sung these songs raucously, cheerfully, mournfully and sentimentally.

They reflect his robust attitude to sex, his affectionate twitting of sergeant-majors, his humour and his resilience. They have echoed from Italy to India, handed down from generation to generation of footslogging fighting men, relieving his weariness and boosting his morale.

Here in this splendid collection they are preserved for posterity.

Hugh de Witt has also edited these collections of limericks old and new:

THERE WAS A YOUNG LADY   Tandem edition 5/–
THERE WAS A FAIR MAID   Tandem edition 5/–

This book is sold subject to the condition that it shall not, by way of trade, be lent, re-sold, hired out or otherwise disposed of without the publisher's consent, in any form of binding or cover other than that in which it is published.

Bawdy Barrack-room Ballads

Hugh de Witt

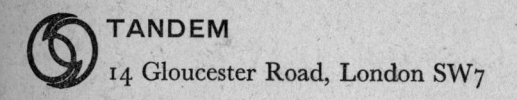

TANDEM
14 Gloucester Road, London SW7

First published in Great Britain by
Universal-Tandem Publishing Co. Ltd, 1970

Copyright © Hugh de Witt 1970

Made and printed in Great Britain by
The Garden City Press Ltd, Letchworth, Herts.

Contents

The Fortunes of War	7
The Fortunes of Peace	7
Preface	8
Apres la Guerre	9
The Australian Poem	10
The Bells of Hell	12
The Bleedin' Sparrer	13
Bring Back	15
Captain Hall	17
Christmas Day in the Workhouse	24
Dan	25
Do Your Balls Hang Low?	26
Don't Dip your Wick in a W.A.C.	27
Eff 'Em All	28
Epitaph For a Biby	29
Epitaph For a Marf	30
The Fair Maid of Amsterdam	31
The Foggy, Foggy Dew	32
Frankie and Johnny	33
Fred Karno's Army	38
The Good Ship Venus	39
Here's To the Good Old Beer	44
I Didn't Want to Join the Army	47
I Lost My . . .	49
I Wore a Tunic	50
In Bloody Orkney	51
In Her Alice-blue Gown	53
In Mobile	54
In the Shade of the Old Apple Tree	55
John Brown's Baby	56
Les Cocottes de la Ville de Marseille	57
Life Presents a Dismal Picture	58
A German Officer Crossed the Line	63
Mademoiselle from Armenteers	71

Some Uncomplimentary Verses	79
Some Rivals	85
The Sergeant-Major's Having a Time	87
Maharajah Mahroo	89
My Nelly	92
Nellie 'Awkins	93
No Balls At All	94
Oh, Bloody, Bloody, Bloody	95
Oh, Give Me a Home	96
The Old Black Bull	97
Old King Cole	99
The Orderly Sergeant	100
Over There	101
The Quartermaster's Stores	103
Raining	110
Recitation	112
Roll Me Over in the Clover	113
Rye Whisky	116
The Sexual Life of the Camel	121
The Sexual Life of the Dodo	122
She Married a Man	123
She was Poor, But She was Honest	124
Tell Us Another One, Do	127
Tiddleywinks, Old Man	138
The Trooper Watering his Nag	139
Twenty Toes	142
Two Toasts	143
The Village Blacksmith	144
We Are the Boys	145
We're Here Because	146
We've Had No Duff	147
When This Bloody War is Over	149
The Woodpecker Song	150
Yoho	152
The Young Harlot of Crete	157
Index of First Lines	158

The Fortunes of War

The fortunes of war
I tell you plain
Are a wooden leg
Or a golden chain.

The Fortunes of Peace

The fortunes of peace
I tell you straight
Are a swollen ball
Or a tax rebate.

PREFACE

BAWDY BARRACK-ROOM BALLADS is an anthology of songs, recitations and limericks popular with British and allied soldiers of two World Wars. The ribaldry of the fighting man sometimes has a coarse cruelty about it, which we would do wrong to take at face value. Not wishing to boast about his bravery, he sings of alleged cowardly follies; restricting sentiment to the privacy of coat pocket, kit-bag, or the letter home, he parades a blatant bawdiness. But always the bawdiness is transmogrified by the injection of that kind of lusty nonsense that is the main characteristic of the English limerick, and which would mock out of sight any tendency to lasciviousness, if such existed.

War is a tense and nasty business and the English-speaking soldier has long ago discovered in bawdy song and recitation an effective safety valve for knotted feelings.

It is important that these songs should be preserved in an anthology such as this, for there are signs that the universality and ready availability of the pop song are putting an end to the specifically army song—if, indeed, they have not already done so. This writer's inquiries round the camps showed that the current Top Twenty has supplanted the traditional army favourites. An additional factor is that wives are more and more invading what was formerly solely male territory, including the mess.

Après la Guerre

> Sung to the tune of the French song,
> 'Sous les ponts de Paris'.

Après la guerre finie,
Soldat anglais parti;
Mademoiselle Fransay boko pleuray
Après la guerre finie.

Après la guerre finie,
Soldat anglais parti;
Mademoiselle in the family way,
Après la guerre finie.

Après la guerre finie,
Soldat anglais parti;
Mademoiselle can go to hell,
Après la guerre finie.

The Australian Poem

A sunburnt bloody stockman stood,
And in a dismal, bloody mood
Apostrophised his bloody cuddy:
'This bloody moke's no bloody good,
He doesn't earn his bloody food.
Bloody! Bloody! Bloody!'

He leapt upon his bloody horse
And galloped off, of bloody course.
The road was wet and bloody muddy;
It led him to the bloody creek;
The bloody horse was bloody weak.
Bloody! Bloody! Bloody!

He said: 'This bloody horse must swim
The same for me as bloody him!'
The creek was deep and bloody floody;
So ere they reached the bloody bank
The bloody steed beneath him sank,
The stockman's face a bloody study,
Ejaculating: 'Bloody! Bloody! Bloody!'

When it came to swearing the British Tommy during the First World War had one superior—the Aussie Trooper. *Bloody* had been a favourite Australian swear word for many years before the war, and the above lines current during World War I were a variant of a satirical poem, entitled *The Great Australian Adjective*, written by the Australian wit W. T. Goodge, and published in the *Sydney Bulletin* in 1899. There had been correspondence in the newspaper at that time on Australia's favourite swear word. It began when Edward E. Morris, author of *Austral English: A Dictionary of Australian Words, Phrases, and Usages,* was given an honorary degree of Doctor of Literature by the University of Melbourne. Melbourne students staged a mock ceremony in which Morris's impersonator was seen to be carrying a large book entitled *The Great Australian Adjective*. What had galled the students was the prudish omission of 'bloody' from Morris's book. (See the Second World War song, *Oh, Bloody, Bloody, Bloody,* and comments, page 95).

The Bells of Hell

Air : Salvation Army Song

The bells of hell go ting-a-ling-a-ling
For you but not for me;
And the little devils how they sing-a-ling-a-ling
For you but not for me.
O Death, where is thy sting-a-ling-a-ling?
O Grave, thy victory?
The bells of hell go ting-a-ling-a-ling
For you but not for me.

The Bleed'n' Sparrer

We 'ad a bleed'n' sparrer wot
Lived up a bleed'n' spaht.
One day the bleed'n' rain came down
An' washed the bleeder aht.

An' as 'e layed 'arf drahned
Dahn in the bleed'n' street,
'E begged that bleed'n' rainstorm
To bave 'is bleed'n' feet.

But then the bleed'n' sun came aht,
Dried up the bleed'n' rain,
So that bleed'n' little sparrer
'E climbed up 'is spaht again.

But, Oh! the crewel sparrer 'awk
'E spies 'im in 'is snuggery,
'E sharpens up 'is bleed'n' claws
An' rips 'im aht by thuggery.

Just then a bleed'n' sportin' type,
Wot 'ad a bleed'n' gun,
'E spots that bleed'n' sparrer 'awk
An' blasts 'is bleed'n' fun.

The moral of this story
Is plain to everyone—
That them wots up the bleed'n' spaht
Don't get no bleed'n' fun.

Bring Back

Sung to the well-known Scottish air

My brother lies over the ocean,
My sister lies over the sea,
My father lies over my mother—
And that's how they got little me.

Chorus:
  Bring back, bring back,
  Oh bring back my Bonnie to me, to me.
  Bring back, bring back,
  Oh bring back my Bonnie to me.

My one skin lies over my two skin,
My two skin lies over my three,
My three skin lies over my foreskin,
So pull back my foreskin for me.

Pull back, pull back,
Oh pull back my foreskin for me, for me.
Pull back, pull back,
Oh pull back my foreskin for me.

A variant used to be sung with great feeling by the cavalry.

Bring back, bring back,
Oh bring back my stirrups to me, to me.
Bring back, bring back,
Oh bring back my stirrups to me.

Bring back, bring back,
I stuck it as long as I could, I could.
Bring back, bring back,
For my ballocks are not made of wood.

Captain Hall

My name is Captain Hall,
Captain Hall.
My name is Captain Hall,
Captain Hall.
My name is Captain Hall,
And I've only got one ball;
But it's better than none at all,
Damn your eyes!
Blast your soul!
But it's better than none at all,
Damn your eyes!

My name is Captain Hall,
Captain Hall.
My name is Captain Hall,
Captain Hall,
My name is Captain Hall,
And I've only got one ball;
The other's mounted on the wall,
Damn your eyes!
Blast your soul!
The other's mounted on the wall,
Damn your eyes!

They say I killed a man,
Killed a man.
They say I killed a man,
Killed a man.
I hit him on the head
With a bloody lump of lead;
And now the fellow's dead,
Damn his eyes!
Blast his soul!
And now the fellow's dead,
Damn his eyes!

They say I killed my wife,
Killed my wife.
They say I killed my wife,
Killed my wife.
But it wasn't with a knife;
No, it wasn't with a knife
That I killed my bloody wife,
Damn her eyes!
Blast her soul!
No, it wasn't with a knife,
Damn her eyes!

The judge's name was Snick,
Name was Snick.
The judge's name was Snick,
Name was Snick.
Said: 'You killed her with your prick,
And we'll hang you very quick;
Yes, we'll hang you very quick,
Damn your eyes!
Blast your soul!
Yes, we'll hang you very quick,
Damn your eyes!'

And now I'm in a cell,
In a cell.
And now I'm in a cell,
In a cell.
And now I'm in a cell,
And ****ing off to Hell;
Perhaps it's just as well,
Damn yer eyes!
Blast yer soul!
Perhaps it's just as well,
Damn yer eyes!

The Chaplain he has come,
He has come.
The Chaplain he has come,
He has come.
The Chaplain he has come,
And he looks so bloomin' glum;
He can kiss my bloody bum,
Damn his eyes!
Blast his soul!
He can kiss my bloody bum,
Damn his eyes!

Now this is my last knell,
My last knell.
Now this is my last knell,
My last knell.
Now this is my last knell,
And you've had a ****ing sell,
For I'll meet you all in hell,
Damn yer eyes!
Blast yer soul!
For I'll meet you all in hell,
Damn yer eyes!

To the gallows I now go,
I now go.
To the gallows I now go,
I now go.
To the gallows I now go,
And the bastards down below,
Think it all a jolly show,
Damn their eyes!
Blast their soul!
Think it all a jolly show,
Damn their eyes!

I see Susie in the crowd,
In the crowd.
I see Susie in the crowd,
In the crowd.
I see Susie in the crowd,
And I 'oller right out loud:
'**** yer, Susie, ain't yer proud?
Damn yer eyes!
Blast yer soul!
**** yer, Susie, ain't yer proud?
 Damn yer eyes!'

Now I feel the rope,
Feel the rope.
Now I feel the rope,
Feel the rope.
Now I feel the rope,
And I've lost all earthly hope;
Nothing but the Chaplain's soap,
Damn his eyes!
Blast his soul!
Nothing but the Chaplain's soap,
Damn his eyes!

Now I am in Hell,
Am in Hell.
Now I am in Hell,
Am in Hell.
Now I am in Hell,
And it's all a ****ing sell,
'Cos the Chaplain's here as well,
Damn his eyes!
Blast his soul!
'Cos the Chaplain's here as well,
Damn his eyes!

This song has an interesting history. It is a variant of an eighteenth-century ballad called *Jack Hall*. He was a chimney-sweep who was hanged for murder. His story was told in one of the ballad-sheets of the day. The Victorian entertainer, W. G. Ross (known as 'The Great Ross') sang it as *Sam Hall*, with some embellishments, in such popular singing taverns of London as the 'Cider Cellars' and the 'Coal Hole'. Ross had a reputation for bawdiness and blasphemy.

When an eightieth-birthday tribute was paid to Charles Morton, who had kept the Canterbury Music Hall, Mrs Beerbohm Tree recited a laudatory poem which began:

>Sixty or seventy years ago,
>In the days of the drinking den,
>The jokes they made,
>And the songs they sang,
>Were sorrow to Englishmen.
>If you doubt my word,
>Take Thackeray down,
>And Colonel Newcome call,
>To tell the tale of the days of Ross,
>And then shudder at vile *Sam Hall*.

When the troops began to sing the song during the First World War they changed the central character to *Captain Hall*.

It is recited or sung in mock-sinister tones.

Christmas Day in the Workhouse

It was Christmas Day in the workhouse,
The season of good cheer:
The paupers' hearts were merry,
Their bellies full of beer.
The pompous workhouse master,
As he strode about the halls,
Called out: 'A Merry Christmas!'
But the paupers answered: 'Balls!'

This angered the workhouse master,
Who swore by all the gods
That he'd stop their Christmas pudden,
The dirty rotten sods!
Then up spake a bald-headed pauper,
His face as bold as brass:
'You can keep your Christmas pudden,
And stick it up your arse!'

Like *'She Was Poor But She Was Honest'*, an example of biting working-class satire.

Dan

Dan, Dan the sanitary man.
Working underground all day.
Cleaning up urinals,
Picking out the 'finals',*
Whiling the happy hours away—
Gor Blimey!

Doing his little bit,
Shovelling up the shit,
He is so blithe and gay.
And the only music that he hears
Is poo-poo-poo-poo-poo all day.

---

*Final editions of evening newspapers, giving the full day's sports results.

Do Your Balls Hang Low?

Do your balls hang low?
Do they dangle to and fro?
Can you tie them in a knot?
Can you tie them in a bow?
Do they itch when it's hot?
Do you rest them in a pot?
Do you get them in a tangle?
Do you catch them in the mangle?
Do they swing in stormy weather?
Do they tickle with a feather?
Do they rattle when you walk?
Do they jingle when you talk?
Can you sling 'em o'er your shoulder
Like a lousy ****ing soldier?
Do your balls hang low?

Sung in a melancholy monotone.

Don't Dip Your Wick in a W.A.C.

Don't dip your wick in a W.A.C.
Don't ride the breast of a W.A.V.E.
   Just sit on the sand
   And do it by hand
And buy bonds with the money you save.

Eff 'em All

Eff 'em all, eff 'em all,
The long and the short and the tall;
Eff all the sergeants and W.O. ones,
Eff all the corporals and their bastard sons;
For we're saying goodbye to 'em all,
As back to our billets we crawl.
You'll get no promotion this side of the ocean,
So cheer up, my lads, eff 'em all.

Epitaph For a Biby

A muvver was barfin' 'er biby one night,
The youngest of ten and a tiny young mite.
The muvver was pore and the biby was thin,
Only a skeleton covered in skin.
The muvver turned round for the soap off the rack;
She was but a moment, but when she turned back
The biby was gorn; and in anguish she cried:
'Oh, where is my biby?'—The angels replied:

'Your biby 'as fell dahn the plug-'ole,
Your biby 'as gorn dahn the plug.
The poor little thing was so skinny and thin
'E oughter been barfed in a jug.
Your biby is perfectly 'appy,
'E won't need a barf any more.
Your biby 'as fell dahn the plug-'ole,
Not lorst, but gorn before.'

Epitaph For a Marf

Wot a marf 'e'd got,
Wot a marf.
When 'e wos a kid,
Goo' Lor' 'luv'll,
'Is pore old muvver
Must 'a' fed 'im wiv a shuvvle.

Wot a gap 'e'd got,
Pore chap.
'E'd never been known to larf;
'Cos if 'e did,
It's a penny to a quid
'E'd 'a' split 'is fice in 'arf.

The Fair Maid of Amsterdam

In Amsterdam there dwelt a maid,
Mark well what I do say;
In Amsterdam there dwelt a maid,
And she was mistress of her trade.

And I'll go no more a-****ing
With you, fair maid.
A-****ing, a-****ing,
Since ****ing's been my ru-i-n,
I'll go no more a-****ing
With you, fair maid.

Her bum was pink, her q**m was brown,
Mark well what I do say;
Her bum was pink, her q**m was brown,
Her hair like glow-worms hanging down.

And I'll go no more a-****ing
With you, fair maid.
A-****ing, a-****ing,
Since ****ing's been my ru-i-n,
I'll go no more a-****ing
With you fair maid.

The Foggy, Foggy Dew

When I was a bachelor I lived by myself,
And I worked at the weaver's trade.
The only, only thing that I ever did wrong
Was to woo a fair young maid.
I wooed her in the winter time,
And in the summer too,
And the only, only thing that I ever did wrong
Was to keep her from the foggy, foggy dew.

One night she came to my bedside
Where I lay fast asleep;
She laid her head upon my bed,
And then began to weep.
She sighed, she cried, she damn near died,
She said: 'What shall I do?'
So I hauled her into bed and I covered up her head,
Just to save her from the foggy, foggy dew.

Oh, I am a bachelor, I live with my son,
And we work at the weaver's trade;
And every, every time that I look into his eyes,
He reminds me of that fair young maid.
He reminds of the winter time,
And of the summer too;
And the many, many times that I held her in my arms,
Just to keep her from the foggy, foggy dew.

Frankie and Johnny

Frankie and Johnny were lovers.
O my Gawd how they did love!
They swore to be true to each other,
As true as the stars above.
He was her man, but he did her wrong.

Frankie and Johnny went walking,
Johnny in a brand new suit.
Frankie went walking with Johnny,
Said: 'O Gawd, don't my Johnny look cute!'
He was her man, but he done her wrong.

Frankie went down to Memphis,
Went on the morning train,
Paid a hundred dollars,
Bought Johnny a watch and chain.
He was her man, but he done her wrong.

Frankie lived in a crib-house,
Crib-house with only two doors,
Gave her money to Johnny,
He spent it on those parlour whores.
He was her man, but he done her wrong.

Frankie went down to the hock-shop,
Went for a bucket of beer,
Said: 'O Mr. Bartender,
Has my loving Johnny been here?
He is my man, but he's doing me wrong.'

'I don't want to make you no trouble,
I don't want to tell you no lie,
But I saw Johnny an hour ago
With a girl named Nelly Bly.
He is your man, but he's doing you wrong.'

Frankie went down to the hotel.
She didn't go down there for fun,
'Cause underneath her kimono
She toted a forty-four gun.
He was her man, but he done her wrong.

Frankie went down to the hotel.
She rang the front-door bell,
Said: 'Stand back all you chippies
Or I'll blow you all to hell.
I want my man, for he's doing me wrong.'

Frankie looked in through the key-hole
And there before her eye
She saw her Johnny on the sofa
A-loving up Nelly Bly.
He was her man; he was doing her wrong.

Frankie threw back her kimono,
Took out a big forty-four.
Root-a-toot-toot, three times she shoot
Right through that hardware door.
He was her man, but was doing her wrong.

Johnny grabbed up his Stetson,
Said: 'O my Gawd, Frankie, don't shoot!'
But Frankie pulled hard on the trigger
And the gun went root-a-toot-toot.
She shot her man, who was doing her wrong.

'Roll me over easy,
Roll me over slow.
Roll me over on my right side
'Cause my left side hurts me so.
I was her man, but I done her wrong.'

Johnny he was a gambler.
He gambled for the gain.
The very last words he ever said
Were: 'High-low Jack and the game.'
He was her man, but he done her wrong.

'Bring out your rubber-tyred buggy,
Bring out your rubber-tyred hack:
I'll take my Johnny to the graveyard
But I won't bring him back.
He was my man, but he done me wrong.'

'Lock me in that dungeon,
Lock me in that cell,
Lock me where the north-east wind
Blows from the corner of Hell.
I shot my man, 'cause he done me wrong.'

Frankie went down to the Madame,
She went down on her knees.
'Forgive me, Mrs Halcombe,
Forgive me if you please
For shooting my man 'cause he done me wrong.'

'Forgive you, Frankie darling,
Forgive you I never can;
Forgive you, Frankie darling,
For shooting your only man.
For he was your man, though he done you
    wrong.'

It was not murder in the first degree,
It was not murder in the third.
A woman simply shot her man
As a hunter drops a bird.
She shot her man, 'cause he done her wrong.

Frankie said to the Sheriff:
'What do you think they'll do?'
The Sheriff said to Frankie:
'It's the electric chair for you.
You shot your man, 'cause he done you wrong.'

Frankie sat in the jail-house,
Had no electric fan,
Told her little sister:
'Don't you marry no sporting man.
I had a man, but he done me wrong.'

Frankie heard a rumbling,
Away down in the ground;
Maybe it was little Johnny
Where she had shot him down.
He was her man, but he done her wrong.

Once more I saw Frankie:
She was sitting in the chair,
Waiting for to go to meet her God,
With the sweat dripping out of her hair.
He was her man, but he done her wrong.

This story has no moral,
This story has no end;
This story only goes to show
That there ain't no good in men.
He was her man, but he done her wrong.

Fred Karno's Army

Sung to the tune of 'The Church's One Foundation'.

> We are Fred Karno's army,
> The ragtime infantry.
> We cannot fight, we cannot shoot,
> What earthly use are we!
>
> And when we get to Berlin,
> The Kaiser he will say,
> 'Hoch, hoch! Mein Gott!
> What a bloody fine lot
> Are the ragtime infantry!'

The Good Ship Venus

The good ship's name was Venus,
Her mast a towering penis,
Her figurehead
A whore in bed—
A jolly sight, by Jesus!

The Captain's name was Slugger,
A filthy rotten bugger.
He wasn't fit
To shovel shit
On any bugger's lugger.

The First Mate's name was Andy.
By God, he was a dandy!
They broke his cock
With lumps of rock
For pissing in the brandy.

The Second Mate's name was Morgan,
By God, he was a Gorgon.
Ten times a day
Fine tunes he'd play
On his reproductive organ.

The Third Mate's name was Paul,
He only had one ball.
But with that knacker
He'd roll terbaccer
Around the cabin wall.

The cabin-boy was Kipper,
A cunning little nipper.
He stuffed his arse
With broken glass
And circumcised the skipper.

Able-Seaman Bowen's
Pecker kept growin' and growin';
It grew so tremendous,
So long and so pendulous,
It was no good for peckin'—just showin'.

The Captain's wife was Alice
And simply out of malice
They'd fill her bum
To the bung with rum
And use her c**t like a chalice.

The Captain's daughter Mabel
They screwed when they were able.
They nailed her tits—
The dirty shits!—
Upon the Captain's table.

The Captain's other daughter
They threw her in the water.
They could tell by the squeals
That some of the eels
Had found her genital quarter.

The Boatswain's name was Lester,
A dirty hymen tester.
Through hymens thick
He bored his prick,
And left it there to fester.

The cook his name was Freeman,
He was a dirty demon.
He fed the crew
On menstrual stew
And hymens fried in semen.

The ship's dog's name was Rover,
The whole crew did him over.
That faithful hound
They ground and ground
From Singapore to Dover.

A talented sailor was Paul,
He was able to bounce either ball.
He'd stretch and snap 'em,
Juggle and clap 'em,
Winning the cheers of them all.

The Captain's treasure, Mabel,
She'd often sprawl on a table,
And cry to her man:
'Stuff in all you can—
Get both balls in if you're able!'

Able-Seaman Hales
Was expert at pissing in gales:
He could piss in a jar
From the top-gallant spar
Without even wetting the sails.

Able-Seaman Long
Was always fondling his dong.
Each time he'd come
He'd loosen his bum,
But couldn't tell s***e from wrong.

For forty days and forty nights
They sailed the broad Atlantic;
And never to pass
A piece of arse
It drove the men quite frantic.

For sixty days and sixty nights
They sailed the broad Pacific;
They'd taken on whores
With good clean bores—
The men said it was terrific.

While in the Adriatic,
Where the water's almost static,
The rise and fall
Of rod and ball
Was almost automatic.

A homo was the purser,
He couldn't have been worser.
He'd screw and screw
With all the crew
Until they yelled: 'No more, sir!'

In search for new sensation,
Amid cries of jubilation,
The ship was sunk
In a wave of spunk
From mutual masturbation.

Here's To the Good Old Beer

Here's to the good old beer,
Mop it down, mop it down!
Here's to the good old beer,
Mop it down!
Here's to the good old beer,
That never leaves you queer,
Here's to the good old beer,
Mop it down!

Here's to the good old whisky,
Mop it down, mop it down!
Here's to the good old whisky,
Mop it down!
Here's to the good old whisky,
That makes you feel so frisky,
Here's to the good old whisky,
Mop it down!

Here's to the good old porter,
Mop it down, mop it down!
Here's to the good old porter,
Mop it down!
Here's to the good old porter,
That slips down like it oughter,
Here's to the good old porter,
Mop it down!

Here's to the good old stout,
Mop it down, mop it down!
Here's to the good old stout,
Mop it down!
Here's to the good old stout,
That makes you feel blown-out,
Here's to the good old stout,
Mop it down!

Here's to the good old port,
Mop it down, mop it down!
Here's to the good old port,
Mop it down!
Here's to the good old port,
That makes you feel a sport,
Here's to the good old port,
Mop it down!

Here's to the good old gin,
Mop it down, mop it down!
Here's to the good old gin,
Mop it down!
Here's to the good old gin,
That fills one up with sin,
Here's to the good old gin,
Mop it down!

Here's to the good old brandy,
Mop it down, mop it down!
Here's to the good old brandy,
Mop it down!
Here's to the good old brandy,
That makes one feel so randy,
Here's to the good old brandy,
Mop it down!

Here's to the good old rum,
Mop it down, mop it down!
Here's to the good old rum,
Mop it down!
Here's to the good old rum,
That warms both balls and bum,
Here's to the good old rum,
Mop it down!

I Didn't Want to Join the Army

I didn't want to join the army;
I didn't want to go to war;
I'd rather have stayed at home,
Round London's streets to roam,
Livin' on the earnin's of an 'igh-class whore.

Chorus
They could have called up me brother,
Me sister and me mother—
But they bleed'n' well called up me!

I don't need no Froggy women;
London's full of girls I never 'ad—
I'd rather have stayed in Blighty—
Lord Gawd Almighty!—
Followin' in the footsteps of me Dad.

Chorus

I didn't want to join the army;
I didn't want to go to war;
I just wanted to to-and-fro
Around the old Soho,
Livin' on the earnin's of an 'igh-class whore.

Chorus

I don't want a bayonet up me arse-whole;
I don't want me ballocks shot away—
I'd rather live in England,
In merry, merry England,
And f**k my bleed'n' life away.

Chorus

A parody of a song, *On Sunday I Walk Out With a Soldier*, which was sung in the revue, *The Passing Show of 1914*.

I Lost My ...

I lost my arm in the army,
I lost my leg in the navy.
I lost my balls over Niagara Falls,
And I lost my cock in a lady.

I Wore a Tunic

Air : 'I Wore a Tulip'

I wore a tunic,
A dirty khaki tunic,
And you wore civilian clothes.
We fought and bled at Loos,
While you were on the booze,
The booze that no one here knows.

Oh, you were with the wenches,
While we were in the trenches,
Facing our German foe.
Oh, you were a-slacking,
While we were attacking
Down on the Menin Road.

The bitterness of the men in the front line for those who dodged military service is voiced in this song.

In Bloody Orkney

This bloody town's a bloody cuss—
No bloody trains, no bloody bus,
And no one cares for bloody us,
In bloody Orkney.

The bloody roads are bloody bad,
The bloody folks are bloody mad,
They'd make the brightest bloody sad,
In bloody Orkney.

All bloody clouds, and bloody rains,
No bloody kerbs, no bloody drains,
The Council's got no bloody brains,
In bloody Orkney.

Everything's so bloody dear,
A bloody bob, for bloody beer,
And is it good—no bloody fear,
In bloody Orkney.

The bloody 'flicks' are bloody old,
The bloody seats are bloody cold
You can't get in for bloody gold,
In bloody Orkney.

The bloody dances make you smile,
The bloody band is bloody vile,
It only cramps your bloody style,
In bloody Orkney.

No bloody sport, no bloody games,
No bloody fun; the bloody dames
Won't even give their bloody names
In bloody Orkney.

Best bloody place is bloody bed,
With bloody ice on bloody head,
You might as well be bloody dead,
In bloody Orkney.

A fuller and more rounded version of the Australian protest in Newfoundland (p. 95) attributed to Captain Hamish Blair.

Ashley Montagu, in his book *The Anatomy of Swearing* (Rapp and Whiting, London, 1968) traces the history of 'bloody' and shows that it was a perfectly respectable word, meaning 'exceedingly' or 'very', until taken over and used in excess as a swear word by the English masses in the early nineteenth century. It became the favourite adjective of the English proletariat, who were not loath to use it to annoy those who claimed to be their 'betters'.

In Her Alice-Blue Gown

In her sweet little Alice-blue gown
Was the first time she ever laid down:
She was both proud and shy
As she opened his fly
And the moment she saw it
She thought she would die.

Oh, it hung almost down to the ground
As it went in it made a sweet sound:
The more that he shoved it
The more that she loved it—
Till he came on her Alice-blue gown.

In Mobile

Oh, the men they wash the dishes, in Mobile.
Oh, the men they wash the dishes, in Mobile.
Oh, the men they wash the dishes
And they dry them on their britches,
Oh, the dirty sons-of-bitches, in Mobile.

Oh, the cows they all are dead, in Mobile.
Oh, the cows they all are dead, in Mobile.
Oh, the cows they all are dead,
So they milk the bulls instead,
Because babies must be fed, in Mobile.

Oh, they teach the babies tricks, in Mobile.
Oh, they teach the babies tricks, in Mobile.
Oh, they teach the babies tricks
And by the time that they are six
They suck their father's pricks, in Mobile.

Oh, there's a shortage of good whores, in Mobile.
Oh, there's a shortage of good whores, in Mobile.
Oh, there's a shortage of good whores,
And men make do with holes in floors
Until their tools have sores, in Mobile.

In the Shade of the Old Apple Tree

In the shade of the old apple tree
Between two plump legs I could see
A little red spot
With some hair in a knot,
And it looked a fine target to me.

I asked while I tickled her tit
If she thought my big thing would fit.
She said it would do,
So she got a good screw
In the shade of the old apple tree.

In the shade of the old apple tree
I got all that was coming to me.
In the soft dewy grass
I'd a fine piece of arse
From a maiden quite lovely to see.

I could hear the buzz-buzz of the bee
As he sunk his grub hooks into me.
Her arse it was fine,
But you should have seen mine
In the shade of the old apple tree.

John Brown's Baby

Air : 'John Brown's Body'

John Brown's baby's got a pimple on his—SHUSH!
John Brown's baby's got a pimple on his—SHUSH!
John Brown's baby's got a pimple on his—SHUSH!
The poor kid can't sit down.

Les Cocottes de la Ville de Marseille

Les cocottes de la ville de Marseille
Sont brunettes de l'ardent soleil.
   Elles pissant du vin blanc
    Couchent pour dix francs—
Mais où sont les patentes de santé?

Life Presents a Dismal Picture

Life presents a dismal picture,
Dark and dreary as the tomb:
Father's got an anal stricture,
Mother's got a prolapsed womb.

Sister Susan's been aborted
For the forty-second time,
Brother Bill has been deported
For a homosexual crime.

In a small brown-paper parcel,
Wrapped in a mysterious way,
Is an imitation rectum
Grandpa uses twice a day.

Jill has chronic menstruation,
Never laughs and never smiles.
Mine's a dismal occupation,
Cracking ice for Grandma's piles.

Cousin Peter's got paresis,
Little Jennie cannot play.
Uncle Joe converses with Jesus,
And says: 'I'm Queen of the May!'

Even now the baby's started,
Having epileptic fits:
Every time it coughs it farts,
Every time it farts it shits.

My balls have become quite painful,
My sphincter's going by degrees.
Paroxysmal incontinence
Brings on quite unasked-for pees.

Now the boxer's got the rabies
Tries to bite us all the time.
The Vicar's wife now has tabes—
Ain't it all a bleedin' shime?

Yet we are not broken-hearted,
Neither are we up the spout.
Auntie Rachel has just farted,
Blown her arsehole inside out.

Sung in the most dolorous manner possible.

The History of Mademoiselle

Strictly speaking, *Mademoiselle From Armenteers* is not one song, but a collection of songs. Its genealogy is composed of many strands and difficult to unravel.

In the pages to follow one close forerunner, *A German Officer Crossed the Line*, precedes the verses of *Mademoiselle*. As we shall see in *The Trooper Watering His Nag* (p. 139) soldiers' songs about landladies' daughters have a long tradition, but a key figure in the story of this one must be Johann Ludwig Uhland, a German poet who lived from 1787 to 1862. He wrote a ballad about three German soldiers who crossed the Rhine and visited a tavern kept by a certain Frau Wirthin who had a pretty young daughter. To her they addressed two questions: firstly, 'Have you good beer and wine?', and secondly, 'How is your little girl?' In response to the latter question, Frau Wirthin took the soldiers to an adjoining room in which lay her dead daughter. Each of the soldiers declared his love for the girl.

It was a serious and touching ballad, but somehow it lent itself to parody. No less a person than Thackeray contributed this couplet:

> 'My beer and wine is as good as ever,
> My daughter is dead of the scarlet fever.'

When fighting men began to sing the song it took on the bawdiness and misleading callousness that was mentioned in the preface to this book. The 'three German soldiers' sometimes became 'three German officers', and finally 'a German officer', and when the First World War came along 'line' was substituted for 'Rhine'. The 'landlady' had by then become the 'landlord'.

According to Edward Arthur Dolph, there was a British song that had a similar tune and verse structure to *Mademoiselle* and whose refrain went 'skibboo, skibboo, skibboodley-boo', and Eric Partridge, an authority on army songs and slang, mentions a source with the refrain 'skiboo, skiboo, ski-bumpity-bump-skiboo'. The now more established 'inky-pinky, parley vous' developed seemingly from these. The British mainly sing 'inky-pinky', but sometimes 'inky-dinky'. The Americans favour 'hinky-dinky'. Attempts to impose a meaning on these refrains are not rewarding. We would do right to assume that their effect is intended to be musical rather than meaningful. They are rather similar to the scat singing of jazz or on a par, as Eric Partridge has pointed out, with the 'hey nonny noes' of Elizabethan song. They also introduce that element of nonsense that has helped to make the limerick so enduringly popular.

It is worth briefly mentioning, as it has not been done elsewhere, that during the Second World War, and for a time afterwards, the word 'Skiboo' enjoyed popularity in the city of Belfast, Northern Ireland. A worker in the Belfast shipyards, perhaps with memories of the First World War song or having heard it from his father, chalked up SKIBOO WAS HERE on the hull of a ship. A rash of Skiboo *graffiti* followed, spreading fast as rumour over the city's red-brick walls and gables. It can be seen chalked on the wall of an air-raid shelter in which James Mason, portraying a wounded I.R.A. man, took refuge in the successful film *Odd Man Out*. Skiboo had now become a person. There was correspondence in the local papers about the origin of the word.

It would be impossible to trace the strange metamorphosis by which Uhland's dead girl finally became a certain French mademoiselle, coarse in appearance, speech and habit, hard-drinking, tough-talking, loose-living. A surprising heroine (or one of the first non-heroines?), but one immediately adopted by the American troops on their arrival at the battlefront, and to this day *Mademoiselle* is a popular song at 'veteran' reunions in the U.S.A.

The Armenteers of the soldiery is in fact Armentières, a French manufacturing town near the border with Belgium, of about thirty thousand inhabitants, and famous for linen and beer. It acted as a British headquarters and supply centre during the First World War. We can see the bawdiness and callousness of the song in perspective when we realise that Death was then a neighbour to Armentières: nearby was Flanders Field and the Plain of Picardy.

Eric Partridge says that in 1915 a Canadian artilleryman called Gitz Ingraham Rice got up a show which included a 'formal and respectable version' of *Mademoiselle from Armenteers*. The versions sung by the soldiers were far from respectable.

The lasting popularity of *Mademoiselle* can be attributed mainly to three features it shares with the also still popular limerick: a lively metre, rhyme and rhythm, its ribaldry, and the opportunity it offers the poetic tyro for composing additional verses.

A German Officer Crossed the Line

A German officer crossed the line,
Skiboo! Skiboo!
A German officer crossed the line,
Skiboo! Skiboo!
A German officer crossed the line,
He was on the hunt for women and wine,
Skiboo! Skiboo!
Ski-bumpity-bump-skiboo!

He was on the hunt for women and wine,
Skiboo! Skiboo!
He was on the hunt for women and wine,
Skiboo! Skiboo!
He was on the hunt for women and wine,
He ****ed the women and drank the wine,
Ski-bumpity-bump-skiboo!

He came upon a wayside inn,
Skiboo! Skiboo!
He came upon a wayside inn,
Skiboo! Skiboo!
He came upon a wayside inn,
Pissed on the wall and walked right in,
Ski-bumpity-bump-skiboo!

Oh, landlord, have you any good wine?
Skiboo! Skiboo!
Oh, landlord, have you any good wine?
Skiboo! Skiboo!
Oh, landlord, have you any good wine,
Fit for an officer of the line?
Ski-bumpity-bump-skiboo!

Oh, yes, I have some very good wine,
Skiboo! Skiboo!
Oh, yes, I have some very good wine,
Skiboo! Skiboo!
Oh, yes, I have some very good wine,
Fit for an officer of the line,
Ski-bumpity-bump-skiboo!

Oh, landlord, have you a daughter fair?
Skiboo! Skiboo!
Oh, landlord, have you a daughter fair?
Skiboo! Skiboo!
Oh, landlord, have you a daughter fair,
With lily-white breasts and flaxen hair?
Ski-bumpity-bump-skiboo!

Oh, yes, I have a daughter fair,
Skiboo! Skiboo!
Oh, yes, I have a daughter fair,
Skiboo! Skiboo!
Oh, yes, I have a daughter fair,
With lily-white breasts and flaxen hair,
Ski-bumpity-bump-skiboo!

But my fair daughter is far too young,
Skiboo! Skiboo!
But my fair daughter is far too young,
Skiboo! Skiboo!
But my fair daughter is far too young,
To be ****ed about by a son of a gun,
Ski-bumpity-bump-skiboo!

Oh, father, father, I'm not too young,
Skiboo! Skiboo!
Oh, father, father, I'm not too young,
Skiboo! Skiboo!
Oh, father, father, I'm not too young,
I've been to bed with the parson's son,
Ski-bumpity-bump-skiboo!

The German officer took a room,
Skiboo! Skiboo!
The German officer took a room,
Skiboo! Skiboo!
The German officer took a room,
The daughter visited him quite soon,
Ski-bumpity-bump-skiboo!

Quite soon he had her on the bed,
Skiboo! Skiboo!
Quite soon he had her on the bed,
Skiboo! Skiboo!
Quite soon he had her on the bed,
****ed her till her **** was red,
Ski-bumpity-bump-skiboo!

He took her round behind the inn,
Skiboo! Skiboo!
He took her round behind the inn,
Skiboo! Skiboo!
He took her round behind the inn,
In no time at all he had it in,
Ski-bumpity-bump-skiboo!

He pressed her down upon her back,
Skiboo! Skiboo!
He pressed her down upon her back,
Skiboo! Skiboo!
He pressed her down upon her back,
****ed away at her lovely crack,
Ski-bumpity-bump-skiboo!

And then he took her to a shed,
Skiboo! Skiboo!
And then he took her to a shed,
Skiboo! Skiboo!
And then he took her to a shed,
****ed her till she near was dead,
Ski-bumpity-bump-skiboo!

He took her down a leafy lane,
Skiboo! Skiboo!
He took her down a leafy lane,
Skiboo! Skiboo!
He took her down a leafy lane,
****ed her back to life again,
Ski-bumpity-bump-skiboo!

He took her into a shady wood,
Skiboo! Skiboo!
He took her into a shady wood,
Skiboo! Skiboo!
He took her into a shady wood,
****ed her hard and ****ed her good,
Ski-bumpity-bump-skiboo!

He ****ed her up, he ****ed her down,
Skiboo! Skiboo!
He ****ed her up, he ****ed her down,
Skiboo! Skiboo!
He ****ed her up, he ****ed her down,
He **** her all around the town,
Ski-bumpity-bump-skiboo!

He ****ed her out, he ****ed her in,
Skiboo! Skiboo!
He ****ed her out, he ****ed her in,
Skiboo! Skiboo!
He ****ed her out, he ****ed her in,
He ****ed her till she near caved in,
Ski-bumpity-bump-skiboo!

The first three months and all was well,
Skiboo! Skiboo!
The first three months and all was well,
Skiboo! Skiboo!
The first three months and all was well,
The second three months she began to swell,
Ski-bumpity-bump-skiboo!

The third three months and she gave a grunt,
Skiboo! Skiboo!
The third three months and she gave a grunt,
Skiboo! Skiboo!
The third three months and she gave a grunt,
And a little red runt popped out of her ****,
Ski-bumpity-bump-skiboo!

The little red runt he grew and grew,
Skiboo! Skiboo!
The little red runt he grew and grew,
Skiboo! Skiboo!
The little red runt he grew and grew,
He ****ed his mother and his sister too,
Ski-bumpity-bump-skiboo!

The little red runt he went to Hell,
Skiboo! Skiboo!
The little red runt he went to Hell,
Skiboo! Skiboo!
The little red runt he went to Hell,
He ****ed the Devil and his wife as well,
Ski-bumpity-bump-skiboo!

It's a hell of a song that we've just sung,
Skiboo! Skiboo!
It's a hell of a song that we've just sung,
Skiboo! Skiboo!
It's a hell of a song that we've just sung,
The bastard that wrote it ought to be hung,
Ski-bumpity-bump-skiboo!

Mademoiselle from Armenteers

Oh, Mademoiselle from Armenteers,
Parlez-vous.
Oh, Mademoiselle from Armenteers,
Parlez-vous.
You didn't have to know her long,
To find the reason why men went wrong!
Inky-pinky, parlez-vous.

Oh, Mademoiselle from Armenteers,
Parlez-vous.
Oh, Mademoiselle from Armenteers,
Parlez-vous.
She sold her kisses for ten francs each,
Soft and juicy, and sweet as a peach!
Inky-pinky, parlez-vous.

Oh, Mademoiselle from Armenteers,
Parlez-vous.
Oh, Mademoiselle from Armenteers,
Parlez-vous.
I had more fun than I can tell
Beneath the sheets with Mademoiselle!
Inky-pinky, parlez-vous.

Oh, Mademoiselle from Armenteers,
Parlez-vous.
Oh, Mademoiselle from Armenteers,
Parlez-vous.
I fell in love with her at sight
And wanked myself for half of that night!
Inky-pinky, parlez-vous.

Oh, Mademoiselle from Armenteers,
Parlez-vous.
Oh, Mademoiselle from Armenteers,
Parlez-vous.
She'd go to church and say her prayers,
Then make a bee-line for the stairs!
Inky-pinky, parlez-vous.

Oh, Mademoiselle from Armenteers,
Parlez-vous.
Oh, Mademoiselle from Armenteers,
Parlez-vous.
She'd give a wink and cry: *'Oui, oui!*
Let's see what you can do with me!'
Inky-pinky, parlez-vous.

Oh, Mademoiselle from Armenteers,
Parlez-vous.
Oh, Mademoiselle from Armenteers,
Parlez-vous.
When on her bed she sure was fun,
Working her arse like a machine gun!
Inky-pinky, parlez-vous.

Oh, Mademoiselle from Armenteers,
Parlez-vous.
Oh, Mademoiselle from Armenteers,
Parlez-vous.
I ****ed with her, but I ****ed too much,
Today when I walk I use a crutch!
Inky-pinky, parlez-vous.

Oh, Mademoiselle from Armenteers,
Parlez-vous.
Oh, Mademoiselle from Armenteers,
Parlez-vous.
When Mademoiselle was in my arms,
Even War was full of charms!
Inky-pinky, parlez-vous.

Oh, Mademoiselle from Armenteers,
Parlez-vous.
Oh, Mademoiselle from Armenteers,
Parlez-vous.
When Mademoiselle was under me
War was very Heaven to me!
Inky-pinky, parlez-vous.

Oh, Mademoiselle from Armenteers,
Parlez-vous.
Oh, Mademoiselle from Armenteers,
Parlez-vous.
She'd grab your peter and give it a squeeze,
Until it hung down below your knees!
Inky-pinky, parlez-vous.

Oh, Mademoiselle from Armenteers,
Parlez-vous.
Oh, Mademoiselle from Armenteers,
Parlez-vous.
The way Mademoiselle could work her pelvis!
This was long before any sign of Elvis!
Inky-pinky, parlez-vous.

Oh, Mademoiselle from Armenteers,
Parlez-vous.
Oh, Mademoiselle from Armenteers,
Parlez-vous.
She wasn't one for erudition,
But she was good at demolition!
Inky-pinky, parlez-vous.

Oh, Mademoiselle from Armenteers,
Parlez-vous.
Oh, Mademoiselle from Armenteers,
Parlez-vous.
She knocked back the Scotch in all the bars,
That's why she always rolled her R's!
Inky-pinky, parlez-vous.

Oh, Mademoiselle from Armenteers,
Parlez-vous.
Oh, Mademoiselle from Armenteers,
Parlez-vous.
She could hold her drink without a doubt.
She was going strong when I passed out!
Inky-pinky, parlez-vous.

Oh, Mademoiselle from Armenteers,
Parlez-vous.
Oh, Mademoiselle from Armenteers,
Parlez-vous.
She wasn't so hot when it came to clothes,
But, God, she had It and This and Those!
Inky-pinky, parlez-vous.

Oh, Mademoiselle from Armenteers,
Parlez-vous.
Oh, Mademoiselle from Armenteers,
Parlez-vous.
She liked them big, did Mademoiselle,
They bigger they came, the harder they fell!
Inky-pinky, parlez-vous.

Oh, Mademoiselle from Armenteers,
Parlez-vous.
Oh, Mademoiselle from Armenteers,
Parlez-vous.
I didn't care what became of me,
That's why I joined the infantry!
Inky-pinky, parlez-vous.

Oh, Mademoiselle from Armenteers,
Parlez-vous.
Oh, Mademoiselle from Armenteers,
Parlez-vous.
Oh, Mademoiselle from Armenteers,
She gave me a lasting souvenir!
Inky-pinky, parlez-vous.

Oh, Mademoiselle from Armenteers,
Parlez-vous.
Oh, Mademoiselle from Armenteers,
Parlez-vous.
The doctor took one look at me
And knew I'd been to Gay Paree!
Inky-pinky, parlez-vous.

Oh, Mademoiselle from Armenteers,
Parlez-vous.
Oh, Mademoiselle from Armenteers,
Parlez-vous.
Her story is sad, it would make you weep,
She fell down a hole and they buried her cheap!
Inky-pinky, parlez-vous.

Oh, Mademoiselle from Armenteers,
Parlez-vous.
Oh, Mademoiselle from Armenteers,
Parlez-vous.
She went down to Hell without delay,
The Devil's still ****ing her every day!
Inky-pinky, parlez-vous.

Oh, Mademoiselle from Armenteers,
Parlez-vous.
Oh, Mademoiselle from Armenteers,
Parlez-vous.
If you'd like to meet old Mademoiselle,
Just pack up your kit and go to Hell!
Inky-pinky, parlez-vous.

Some Uncomplimentary Verses

Oh, Mademoiselle from Armenteers,
Parlez-vous.
Oh, Mademoiselle from Armenteers,
Parlez-vous.
She had five chins, her knees would knock,
Her face would stop a cuckoo clock!
Inky-pinky, parlez-vous.

Oh, Mademoiselle from Armenteers,
Parlez-vous.
Oh, Mademoiselle from Armenteers,
Parlez-vous.
Her feet were large as any man's,
Like navvy's spades her huge red hands!
Inky-pinky, parlez-vous.

Oh, Mademoiselle from Armenteers,
Parlez-vous.
Oh, Mademoiselle from Armenteers,
Parlez-vous.
Her legs were thick, like trunks of trees,
Her clitoris dangled to her knees!
Inky-pinky, parlez-vous.

Oh, Mademoiselle from Armenteers,
Parlez-vous.
Oh, Mademoiselle from Armenteers,
Parlez-vous.
Her turnip cheeks were blotched with rouge,
Her arse was large, her c**t was huge!
Inky-pinky, parlez-vous.

Oh, Mademoiselle from Armenteers,
Parlez-vous.
Oh, Mademoiselle from Armenteers,
Parlez-vous.
Turnip tit and crooked nipple,
Shagging her made her belly ripple!
Inky-pinky, parlez-vous.

Oh, Mademoiselle from Armenteers,
Parlez-vous.
Oh, Mademoiselle from Armenteers,
Parlez-vous.
Her paps were dry, her muff was rough,
She did her best with a powder puff!
Inky-pinky, parlez-vous.

Oh, Mademoiselle from Armenteers,
Parlez-vous.
Oh, Mademoiselle from Armenteers,
Parlez-vous.
She had never heard of underwear,
Beneath her skirt was a nest of hair!
Inky-pinky, parlez-vous.

Oh, Mademoiselle from Armenteers,
Parlez-vous.
Oh, Mademoiselle from Armenteers,
Parlez-vous.
Men went to the front and met their death
To get away from her garlic breath!
Inky-pinky, parlez-vous.

Oh, Mademoiselle from Armenteers,
Parlez-vous.
Oh, Mademoiselle from Armenteers,
Parlez-vous.
Her c**t was like a cavern wide,
Two soldiers could play at cards inside!
Inky-pinky, parlez-vous.

Oh, Mademoiselle from Armenteers,
Parlez-vous.
Oh, Mademoiselle from Armenteers,
Parlez-vous.
They screwed her high, they screwed her low,
They screwed her till her bum would glow!
Inky-pinky, parlez-vous.

Oh, Mademoiselle from Armenteers,
Parlez-vous.
Oh, Mademoiselle from Armenteers,
Parlez-vous.
She had not bathed in twenty years,
You could grow tomatoes in her ears!
Inky-pinky, parlez-vous.

Oh, Mademoiselle from Armenteers,
Parlez-vous.
Oh, Mademoiselle from Armenteers,
Parlez-vous.
For a chocolate bar or chewing gum
Any son of a gun could have her bum!
Inky-pinky, parlez-vous.

Oh, Mademoiselle from Armenteers,
Parlez-vous.
Oh, Mademoiselle from Armenteers,
Parlez-vous.
Her age was only twenty and three,
But most times she looked a century!
Inky-pinky, parlez-vous.

Oh, Mademoiselle from Armenteers,
Parlez-vous.
Oh, Mademoiselle from Armenteers,
Parlez-vous.
Her bloomers were old and out of date,
And tight at the bottom—the kind men hate!
Inky-pinky, parlez-vous.

Oh, Mademoiselle from Armenteers,
Parlez-vous.
Oh, Mademoiselle from Armenteers,
Parlez-vous.
She'd readily agree to 'sixty-nine'
With any rotten bastard from the line!
Inky-pinky, parlez-vous.

Oh, Mademoiselle from Armenteers,
Parlez-vous.
Oh, Mademoiselle from Armenteers,
Parlez-vous.
By the light of the evening star,
Her standard price a chocolate bar!
Inky-pinky, parlez-vous.

Oh, Mademoiselle from Armenteers,
Parlez-vous.
Oh, Mademoiselle from Armenteers,
Parlez-vous.
The only thing that she gave free,
The doctors took away from me!
Inky-pinky, parlez-vous.

Some Rivals

Oh, Mademoiselle from Amiens,
Parlez-vous.
Oh, Mademoiselle from Amiens,
Parlez-vous.
Oh, Mademoiselle from Amiens,
She'd never keep her knickers on!
Inky-pinky parlez-vous.

Oh, Mademoiselle from St. Nazaire,
Parlez-vous.
Oh, Mademoiselle from St. Nazaire,
Parlez-vous.
Oh, Mademoiselle from St. Nazaire,
Lift and you'll find her bottom's bare!
Inky-pinky, parlez-vous.

Oh, Mademoiselle from Montparnasse,
Parlez-vous.
Oh, Mademoiselle from Montparnasse,
Parlez-vous.
Oh, Mademoiselle from Montparnasse,
For a chocolate bar she'd bare her ass!
Inky-pinky, parlez-vous.

Oh, Mademoiselle from Old Verdun,
Parlez-vous.
Oh, Mademoiselle from Old Verdun,
Parlez-vous.
Oh, Mademoiselle from Old Verdun,
She'll let you feel her bum for fun!
Inky-pinky, parlez-vous.

Oh, Mademoiselle from Gay Paree,
Parlez-vous.
Oh, Mademoiselle from Gay Paree,
Parlez-vous.
Oh, Mademoiselle from Gay Paree,
She'll let you kiss her bum for free!
Inky-pinky, parlez-vous.

Oh, Mademoiselle from the town of Grasse,
Parlez-vous.
Oh, Mademoiselle from the town of Grasse,
Parlez-vous.
Oh, Mademoiselle from the town of Grasse,
She's got roses growing from her ass!
Inkey-pinky, parlez-vous.

The Sergeant-Major's Having a Time

The sergeant-major's having a time,
Parlez-vous.
The sergeant-major's having a time,
Parlez-vous.
The sergeant-major's having a time,
Swinging the lead behind the line,
Inky-pinky, parlez-vous.

The sergeant-major's having a time,
Parlez-vous.
The sergeant-major's having a time,
Parlez-vous.
The sergeant-major's having a time,
Swigging the beer behind the line,
Inky-pinky, parlez-vous.

The sergeant-major's having a time,
Parlez-vous.
The sergeant-major's having a time,
Parlez-vous.
The sergeant-major's having a time,
Abusing himself behind the line,
Inky-pinky, parlez-vous.

The sergeant-major's having a time,
Parlez-vous.
The sergeant-major's having a time,
Parlez-vous.
The sergeant-major's having a time,
****ing the girls behind the line,
Inky-pinky, parlez-vous.

It was inevitable that the sergeant-major should feature in some of the *Mademoiselle* verses. He is on the receiving end of much army humour. 'Some say Good old sergeant. Others say . . .'

Maharajah Mahroo

Down in the slums of a Rangoon back street
There dwelt one Sunset Sue:
A Jane whose claim to fame was known
From Malay to Timbuctoo.

For Sue had ****ed in every land,
From the Persian Gulf to China;
And the tools of a thousand Eastern kings
Had been through her vagina.

Now one hot day Sue had given way
To a seething surge of lust,
And Sunset Sue after nine months knew
That it was s**t or bust.

So she walked in state to the palace gate
And tore her drawers asunder
And dropped her load on that Burma Road
With a fart like tropic thunder.

Now that little brown bastard she dropped on
 the road
Was the lusty Maharajah Mahroo,
Whose balls were used as cannon shells
At the Aldershot Tattoo;

Whose tool was as long as an Arctic winter,
Black as a Burmese tit,
Harder than doing the Indian rope trick,
Harder than eating s**t.

Now he started to walk though he found it hard
With a tool weighing three stone four,
And the trail of his balls dug a three-foot trench
Through Malay and Singapore.

Now Maharajah Mahroo when he was young
Did earn a precarious fee
For leading blind whores from the brothel doors
Down to the river to pee.

Now Lindy Lou was a mountain whore
From the hills beyond Madras,
With breasts that flowed like mountain springs
And a c**t like the Hell Fire Pass;

A c**t as wide as the Indian Ocean,
Smooth as a pane of glass,
Inlaid with eighteen carat gold
And thatched with pampas grass.

Now the Harlot Queen of Singapore
Was a worn out rusty jade
With a fallen womb and hanging breasts
Like a sandbag barricade.

Now a hundred maids in waiting
Watched him heaving a shining arse
As he pushed the Road to Mandalay
Right through the Hell Fire Pass.

And he leapt at Lou like a lion loose,
Filled with a mad desire,
And Lindy Lou was shitting bricks
At a rapid rate of fire.

And rogering roughly, ****ing fiercely,
Pulsing with Persian passion,
He screwed that whore to the s**thouse door
In oriental fashion.

Now that is the end of Lindy Lou,
For now she lies in state,
With **** all else but a saucepan lid
Carved on the coffin plate.

My Nelly

Air: 'Three Blind Mice'

My Nelly's a whore!
My Nelly's a whore!
She's got such wonderful eyes of blue.
She uses such wonderful language too.
Her favourite expression is: 'Ballocks to you!'
My Nelly's a whore!

Nellie 'Awkins

I first met Nellie 'Awkins
Down the Old Kent Road.
Her drawers were round her knees,
'Cos she'd been with Charlie Lees.
I pressed a filthy tanner
In her filthy bleedin' hand.
'Cos she was a low-down whore.

She wore no blouses
And I wore no trousers,
And she wore no underclothes;
And when she caressed me
She damn near undressed me.
It's a thrill that no one knows.

I went to the doctor.
He said: 'Where did you block 'er?'
I said: 'Down where the green grass grows.'
He said, quick as a twinkle:
'The pimple on your winkle
Will be bigger than a red, red rose.'

Cockney humour has made a major contribution to the song repertoire of the British fighting man.

No Balls At All

Hitler has only got one ball.
Goering has two, but they're too small.
Himmler is something similar,
But poor old Goebbels has no balls at all.

A Second World War favourite, sung to the tune 'Colonel Bogey'.

Oh, Bloody, Bloody, Bloody

No bloody sports;
No bloody games;
No bloody fun
With bloody dames;
Won't even tell
Their bloody names—
Oh, bloody, bloody, bloody!

The lament of Australian troops stationed in Newfoundland during the Second World War. Other troops, in other places, have experienced similar frustrations. Swearing is one way to relieve frustration.

'Bloody' is a British swear word that early established itself in the Australian vocabulary. Alexander Marjoribanks, who travelled in New South Wales in 1847, reported: 'One may tell you that he married a bloody young wife, another, a bloody old one; and a bushranger will call out: "Stop, or I'll blow your bloody brains out".' He heard a bullock driver use 'bloody' twenty-seven times in fifteen minutes, and seemingly being of a mathematical turn of mind estimated that if the driver started swearing at twenty and lived to be seventy he would utter 'this disgusting word no less than 18,200,000 times'.

Oh, Give Me a Home

Oh, give me a home
Where the prostitutes roam,
And your ballocks hang down to your knees.
Where the babies are born
With a fourteen inch horn
And pox is the favourite disease.

The Old Black Bull

The old black bull came down from the mountain,
Euston, Dan Euston.
The old black bull came down from the mountain,
A long time ago.

> *Chorus:*
> *A long time ago.*
> *A long time ago.*
> *The old black bull came down from the mountain,*
> *A long time ago.*

There were six fine heifers in the pasture grazing,
Euston, Dan Euston.
There were six fine heifers in the pasture grazing,
A long time ago.

> *Chorus:*
> *A long time ago.*
> *A long time ago.*
> *There were six fine heifers in the pasture grazing,*
> *A long time ago.*

Now the old bull's gone back to the mountain,
Euston, Dan Euston.
Now the old bull's gone back to the mountain,
A long time ago.

> *Chorus:*
> *A long time ago.*
> *A long time ago.*
> *Now the old bull's gone back to the mountain,*
> *A long time ago.*

And his head hung low and his back was broken,
Euston, Dan Euston.
And his head hung low and his back was broken,
A long time ago.

> *Chorus:*
> *A long time ago.*
> *A long time ago.*
> *And his head hung low and his back was broken,*
> *A long time ago.*

A Somerset song taken into the army repertoire in 1914.

Old King Cole

Old King Cole was a bugger for the hole,
And a bugger for the hole was he.
He called for his wife
In the middle of the night
And he called for his K-N-I-F-E.

Old King Cole was a bugger for the hole,
And a bugger for the hole was he.
He called for his wife
In the middle of the night
And stuck her with his K-N-I-F-E.

Old King Cole was a bugger for the hole,
And a bugger for the hole was he.
He called for his wife
And stuck her with his knife,
And out jumped a K-I-D.

The Orderly Sergeant

The orderly sergeant says:
'Look here, my lad,
You're late on parade
And your turn-out is bad;
I've seen things like you
Behind bars in the zoo.'
Rejoined I: '**** 'em all,
And to begin with,
**** you!'

Over There

Oh, the peters they are small,
Over there.
Oh, the peters they are small,
Over there.
Oh, the peters they are small,
Because they work 'em for a fall,
And then eats 'em, tops and all,
Over there.

Oh, the pussies they are small,
Over there.
Oh, the pussies they are small,
Over there.
Oh, the pussies they are small,
But they take 'em short and tall,
And then burns their pricks and all,
Over there.

Oh, I wish I was a pimp,
Over there.
Oh, I wish I was a pimp,
Over there.
Oh, I wish I was a pimp,
For I'd give the boys a crimp
With all my whorey blimps,
Over there.

Oh, they had a squirt for clap,
Over there.
Oh, they had a squirt for clap,
Over there.
Oh, they had a squirt for clap,
It was potent clap trap,
And it burnt our pecker's cap,
Over there.

The Quartermaster's Stores

There was Andy, Andy, feeling randy dandy,
In the stores, in the stores.
There was Andy, Andy, feeling randy dandy,
In the quartermaster's stores.

> *Chorus:*
> *My eyes are dim, I cannot see,*
> *I have not got my specs with me,*
> *I have not got my specs with me.*

There was Barney, Barney, feeling huge and horney,
In the stores, in the stores.
There was Barney, Barney, feeling huge and horney,
In the quartermaster's stores.

> *Chorus*

There was Cox, Cox, catching a powerful pox,
In the stores, in the stores.
There was Cox, Cox, catching a powerful pox,
In the quartermaster's stores.

> *Chorus*

There was Danny, Danny, putting it into Granny,
In the stores, in the stores.
There was Danny, Danny, putting it into Granny,
In the quartermaster's stores.

Chorus

There was Ellen, Ellen, finding seventh heaven,
In the stores, in the stores.
There was Ellen, Ellen, finding seventh heaven,
In the quartermaster's stores.

Chorus

There was Fritz, Fritz, sucking his sister's tits,
In the stores, in the stores.
There was Fritz, Fritz, sucking his sister's tits,
In the quartermaster's stores.

Chorus

There was George, George, his ballocks swollen large,
In the stores, in the stores.
There was George, George, his ballocks swollen large,
In the quartermaster's stores.

Chorus

There was Hank, Hank, having himself a wank,
In the stores, in the stores.
There was Hank, Hank, having himself a wank,
In the quartermaster's stores.

Chorus

There was Ike, Ike, playing with his spike,
In the stores, in the stores.
There was Ike, Ike, playing with his spike,
In the quartermaster's stores.

Chorus

There was Jock, Jock, going knock, knock, knock,
In the stores, in the stores.
There was Jock, Jock, going knock, knock, knock,
In the quartermaster's stores.

Chorus

There was Kent, Kent, his pecker red and bent,
In the stores, in the stores.
There was Kent, Kent, his pecker red and bent,
In the quartermaster's stores.

Chorus

There was Lil, Lil, lusting for a fill,
In the stores, in the stores.
There was Lil, Lil, lusting for a fill,
In the quartermaster's stores.

Chorus

There was Mabel, Mabel, having it on the table,
In the stores, in the stores.
There was Mabel, Mabel, having it on the table,
In the quartermaster's stores.

Chorus

There was Nelly, Nelly, with a swollen belly,
In the stores, in the stores.
There was Nelly, Nelly, with a swollen belly,
In the quartermaster's stores.

Chorus

There was Ollie, Ollie, climbing on to Mollie,
In the stores, in the stores.
There was Ollie, Ollie, climbing on to Mollie,
In the quartermaster's stores.

Chorus

There were pros, pros, in orgasmic throes,
In the stores, in the stores,
There were pros, pros, in orgasmic throes,
In the quartermaster's stores.

Chorus

There were quails, quails, red beneath their tails,
In the stores, in the stores.
There were quails, quails, red beneath their tails,
In the quartermaster's stores.

Chorus

There was Raines, Raines, leaving filthy stains,
In the stores, in the stores.
There was Raines, Raines, leaving filthy stains,
In the quartermaster's stores.

Chorus

There was shit, shit, lots and lots of shit,
In the stores, in the stores.
There was shit, shit, lots and lots of shit,
In the quartermaster's stores.

Chorus

There were tarts, tarts, exposing private parts,
In the stores, in the stores.
There were tarts, tarts, exposing private parts,
In the quartermaster's stores.

Chorus

There was urine, urine, streams and streams of urine,
In the stores, in the stores.
There was urine, urine, streams and streams of urine,
In the quartermaster's stores.

Chorus

There was Vicky, Vicky, calling out for Dicky,
In the stores, in the stores.
There was Vicky, Vicky, calling out for Dicky,
In the quartermaster's stores.

Chorus

There were whores, whores, with nasty bleeding sores,
In the stores, in the stores.
There were whores, whores, with nasty bleeding sores,
In the quartermaster's stores.

Chorus

There was X, X, lots of lovely X,
In the stores, in the stores.
There was X, X, lots of lovely X,
In the quartermaster's stores.

Chorus

There were Yanks, Yanks, tossing into tanks,
In the stores, in the stores.
There were Yanks, Yanks, tossing into tanks,
In the quartermaster's stores.

Chorus

There was zest, zest, but let's give this song a rest,
In the stores, in the stores.
There was zest, zest, but let's give this song a rest,
In the quartermaster's stores.

Raining

Air: 'Holy, Holy, Holy'

Raining, raining, raining.
Always bloodywell raining.
Raining all the morning,
And raining all the night.

Lousing, lousing, lousing.
Always bloodywell lousing.
Lousing all the morning,
And lousing all the night.

Boozing, boozing, boozing.
Always bloodywell boozing.
Boozing all the morning,
And boozing all the night.

Grousing, grousing, grousing,
Always bloodywell grousing,
Grousing at the rations,
And grousing at the pay.

Marching, marching, marching,
Always bloodywell marching.
Marching all the morning,
And marching all the night.

Marching, marching, marching.
Always bloodywell marching.
When the war is over
We'll damn well march no more!

Recitation

He grabbed me round my slender neck,
I could not shout or scream;
He carried me into his room
Where we could not be seen;
He tore away my flimsy wrap
And gazed upon my form—
I was so cold and still and damp,
While he was wet and warm.
His feverish mouth he pressed to mine—
I let him have his way—
He drained me of my very self;
I could not say him nay.
He made me what I am. Alas!
That's why you find me here . . .
A broken vessel—broken glass—
That once held Bottled Beer.

Roll Me Over in the Clover

Oh, this is number one,
And the fun has just begun.
Roll me over,
Lay me down,
And do it again.

> *Chorus:*
> *Roll me over*
> *In the clover;*
> *Roll me over,*
> *Lay me down,*
> *And do it again.*

Oh, this is number two,
And my hand is on her shoe.
Roll me over,
Lay me down,
And do it again.

> *Chorus*

Oh, this is number three,
And my hand is on her knee.
Roll me over,
Lay me down,
And do it again.

> *Chorus*

Oh, this is number four,
And we're lying on the floor.
Roll me over,
Lay me down,
And do it again.

Chorus

Oh, this is number five,
And we're feeling so alive.
Roll me over,
Lay me down,
And do it again.

Chorus

Oh, this is number six,
And she's swooning at my tricks.
Roll me over,
Lay me down,
And do it again.

Chorus

Oh, this is number seven,
And we feel we're in heaven.
Roll me over,
Lay me down,
And do it again.

Chorus

Oh, this is number eight,
And the nurse is at the gate.
Roll me over,
Lay me down,
And do it again.

Chorus

Oh, this is number nine,
And the twins are doing fine.
Roll me over,
Lay me down,
And do it again.

Chorus

Oh, this is number ten,
And we're at it once again.
Roll me over,
Lay me down,
And do it again.

Chorus

Rye Whisky

I'll eat when I'm hungry,
I'll drink when I'm dry;
If the hard times don't kill me,
I'll lay down and die.

> *Chorus:*
>
> *Rye whisky, rye whisky,*
> *Rye whisky, I cry;*
> *If you don't give me rye whisky,*
> *I surely will die.*

I'll tune up my fiddle,
And I'll rosin my bow,
I'll make myself welcome,
Wherever I go.

> *Chorus*

Beefsteak when I'm hungry,
Red liquor when I'm dry;
Greenbacks when I'm hard up,
And religion when I die.

> *Chorus*

They say I drink whisky,
My money's my own;
All them that don't like me,
Can leave me alone.

Chorus

Sometimes I drink whisky,
Sometimes I drink rum;
Sometimes I drink brandy,
At other times none.

Chorus

But if I get boozy,
My whisky's my own;
And them that don't like me,
Can leave me alone.

Chorus

Jack o' diamonds, jack o' diamonds,
I know you of old;
You've robbed my poor pockets,
Of silver and gold.

Chorus

Oh, whisky, you villain,
You've been my downfall;
You've kicked me, you've cuffed me,
But I love you for all.

Chorus

If the ocean was whisky,
And I was a duck,
I'd dive to the bottom,
To get one sweet suck.

Chorus

But the ocean ain't whisky,
And I ain't a duck,
So we'll round up the cattle,
And then we'll get drunk.

Chorus

My foot's in my stirrup,
My bridle's in my hand;
I'm leaving sweet Lillie,
The fairest in the land.

Chorus

Her parents don't like me,
They say I'm too poor;
They say I'm unworthy
To enter her door.

Chorus

Sweet milk when I'm hungry,
Rye whisky when I'm dry;
If a tree don't fall on me,
I'll live till I die.

Chorus

I'll buy my own whisky,
I'll make my own stew;
If I get drunk, madam,
It's nothing to you.

Chorus

I'll drink my own whisky,
I'll drink my own wine;
Some ten thousand bottles
I've killed in my time.

Chorus

I've no wife to quarrel,
No babies to bawl;
The best way of living
Is no wife at all.

Chorus

Way up on Clinch Mountain
I wander alone;
I'm as drunk as the Devil—
Oh, let me alone!

  Chorus

You may boast of your knowledge
And brag of your sense;
'Twill all be forgotten
A hundred years hence.

  Chorus

The Sexual Life of the Camel

The sexual life of the camel
Is stranger than anyone thinks:
At the height of the mating season
He tries to bugger the sphinx.
But the sphinx's posterior sphincter
Is all clogged by the sands of the Nile,
Which accounts for the hump on the camel
And the sphinx's inscrutable smile.

The Sexual Life of the Dodo

The sexual life of the Dodo
Was stranger than anyone thinks:
At the height of the mating season
He liked to be buggered by Chinks.
But the Dodo's posterior sphincter
Was a very odd shape for to slot,
Which accounts for the Dodo's extinction
And the ——* of the Chinese twat.

*In recitation, drawn with a finger in the air.

She Married a Man

The Squire had a daughter, so fair and so tall,
She lived in her satins and silks at the Hall,
But she married a man who had no balls at all.
  No balls at all,
  No balls at all,
She married a man who had no balls at all.

A close relation of Sam or Captain Hall

She was Poor, But She was Honest

She was poor, but she was honest,
Victim of the squire's whim:
First he wooed her, then seduced her,
And she had a child by him.

> *Chorus:*
> *Oh, it's the sime the whole world over*
> *It's the poor wot gets the blime,*
> *While the rich gets all the grivy—*
> *Ain't it all a bleeding shime?*

Off she went to London city
For to hide her grief and shame:
Another rich man seduced her,
And she lost her name again.

> *Chorus*

In the rich man's arms she fluttered,
Like a bird with broken wing:
First he loved her, then he left her—
And she hadn't got a ring.

> *Chorus*

What right had he with all his money
To discard her that was so poor,
Bring shime on her relations,
Turning her into a whore?

Chorus

See him in his splendid mansion,
Entertaining with the best,
While the girl that he has ruined,
Entertains a sordid guest.

Chorus

See him with his hounds and horses,
See him boasting at his club,
While the victim of his lusting
Sips her gin inside a pub.

Chorus

See him in the grand the-ay-ter,
Watching ballet from the pit,
While the poor girl that he ruined
Trails her way through mud and shit.

Chorus

See him in the House of Commons,
Passing laws to put down crime,
While the victim of his passion,
Has to hide her face in shime.

Chorus

See the little country cottage
Where her broken parents live:
Though they drink the fizz she sends them,
Yet they never can forgive.

Chorus

Standing on the bridge at midnight,
She cries: 'Farewell, blighted love!'
There's a scream, a splash—Good Heavens!
What is she a-doing of?

Chorus

Then they drag her from the river,
Water from her clothes they wrang;
For they thought that she was drownded;
But the corpse got up and sang:

> *'It's the sime the whole world over,*
> *It's the poor wot gets the blime,*
> *While the rich gets all the grivy—*
> *Ain't it all a bleedin' shime?'*

The leading English class-war favourite, to be sung with an exaggerated Cockney accent.

Tell Us Another One, Do

A man in the battle of Aix
Had one nut and his pud shot away;
   But found in this pickle
   His nose could still tickle—
Now he f***s with it, so people say.

   Chorus:
   That was a jolly good rhyme,
   Tell us another one, do.

There was a young army cadet
Whose drawers were unusually wet.
   When he dreamt of his wedding
   He soaked all the bedding—
The weddin' ain't taken place yet.

   Chorus

A prisoner in Château d'If
Ran around on all fours for a sniff
   Of his comrade's posterior
   And said: 'It's inferior,
But somehow it reminds me of quiff.'

   Chorus

A prosperous merchant in Rhône
Took orders for c**t on the phone.
   Or the same could be baled,
   Stamped, labelled, and mailed
To a limited parcel-post zone.

Chorus

There once was a gouty old colonel,
Who grew glum when the weather grew vernal;
   And he cried in his tiffin,
   For his prick wouldn't stiffen—
And the size of the thing was infernal.

Chorus

There once was a Colonel Defoe,
Who went for a ski in the snow.
   He travelled so fast
   That he skimmed off his arse—
And one testicle now has to go.

Chorus

There was a young soldier, McGill,
Who was always seen marching uphill.
   When someone inquired:
   'Good God, ain't you tired?'
He said: 'No, it makes my balls thrill.'

Chorus

There was a young Nazi amoeba,
Who loved a Jewess named Reba.
   This primeval jelly
   Would wiggle up her belly
And gently whisper: 'Ich liebe.'

Chorus

Meat rationing did not terrify Miss Davey.
She got married to a sailor in the navy.
   For she knew between his legs
   He had ham and he had eggs,
A big weenie and oodles of fine gravy.

Chorus

A company of Grenadier Guards
While traversing the park, formed in squads,
    Saw two naked statues
    At three-quarter twat views—
Which perceptibly stiffened their rods.

   Chorus

An old Japanese samurai named Haki
Once pickled his peenie in saki,
    When his thing was quite dead
    He cried with bowed head:
'Banzai! Requiescat in pace!'

   Chorus

The prick of a young man of Kew
Had veins that were azure in hue.
    Its head was quite red
    So he waved it and said:
'Three cheers for the red, white, and blue!'

   Chorus

There's a charming young girl in Tobruk,
Who refers to her quiff as her nook.
   It's deep and it's wide;
   You can curl up inside
With a nice easy chair and a book.

  Chorus

When he tried to inject his huge whanger
A young man aroused his girl's anger.
   As she strove in the dark,
   She was heard to remark:
'What you need is a Zeppelin hangar.'

  Chorus

A very odd pair are the Pitts:
His balls are as big as her tits;
   Each breast is as large
   As an invasion barge—
Neither knows how the other cohabits.

  Chorus

There was an old whore of Marseille,
Who tried a new rotary spray.
   Said she: 'Ah, that's better;
   Why, here's a French letter
That's been missing since Armistice Day.'

Chorus

There was a young man, Mussolini,
Who found he had seven bambini.
   Said he: 'If I'd thought
   The griddle was hot,
I'd never have put in my weenie.'

Chorus

There was a young man from Berlin,
A master of sexual sin.
   He crammed the small crease
   Twixt the legs of his niece
With a foot of his old rolling pin.

Chorus

There was a young man of Jaipur,
Whose J.T. was shot off in the war.
   So he painted the front
   To resemble a c**t
And set himself up as a whore.

Chorus

There was a G.I. name of Snyder,
Who took a girl out just to ride her.
   She allowed him to feel
   From her neck to her heel—
But never would let him inside her.

Chorus

An innocent soldier named Stave,
Was nearly seduced by a W.A.V.E.;
   But he's still a recluse
   With all of his juice,
For he never learned how to behave.

Chorus

There was a young sergeant named Schmidt,
Fond of a crime to commit.
    He thought raping women
    Was frightfully common,
So he buggered an aged Tom Tit.

Chorus

A fanatic gun-lover named Crust
Was perverse to the point of disgust.
    His idea of a peach
    Had a sixteen-inch breech
And a pearl-handled forty-four bust.

Chorus

Said a promiscuous lecherous Nazi:
'Our iocas may sound hotsy-totsy;
    But a girl when we diddle her
    Must keep shouting, "Heil Hitler!"
Though it all seems a trifle eratzy.'

Chorus

A girl of uncertain nativity
Had an arse of extreme sensitivity:
    When she sat on the lap
    Of a German or Jap
She could sense fifth-column activity.

    Chorus

Since donning a uniform, Joe
Quit the floozies he once used to know.
    Says he : 'Sergeant Bennetils
    Now tickles my genitals
Every night at the old U.S.O.'

    Chorus

Said a lusty young soldier named Mickey
As his girl eyed his upstanding dickey:
    'Kid, my leave's almost up
    And I feel like a tup—
Bend down and I'll slip it in quickie.'

    Chorus

Fat old Field-Marshal Goering,
He once bored a hole in the flooring.
   He lined it all round,
   Then lay on the ground,
Declaring: 'It's cheaper than whoring!'

   Chorus

There was an old soldier of Rheims,
Who played with himself in his dreams.
   On his nightshirt in front
   He painted a c**t
Which made his sperm gush forth in streams.

   Chorus

Plump old Colonel Breech-Cantor
Was bloated with bawdy bold banter.
   He'd sit on his ass
   And let fly his gas
Whenever he sniffed a decanter.

   Chorus

A gouty old colonel said: 'Tush!
My balls always hang in the bush,
   And I fumble about,
   Half in and half out,
With a pecker too limber to mush.'

  Chorus

Tiddleywinks, Old Man

Tiddleywinks, Old Man,
Find a woman if you can.
If you can't find a woman,
Do without, Old Man.

When the Rock of Gibraltar
Takes a flying leap at Malta
You'll never get your ballocks in a bully-beef can.

The Trooper Watering His Nag

There was an old woman who lived under a hill,
Sing trolly, lolly, lolly, lo!
She had good beer and ale for to sell:
Ho, ho! Had she so? Had she so? Had she so?

She had a daughter, her name was Siss,
Sing trolly, lolly, lolly, lo!
She kept her at home for to welcome her guest:
Ho, ho! Did she so? Did she so? Did she so?

There came a trooper riding by,
Sing trolly, lolly, lolly, lo!
He called for a drink most plentifully:
Ho, ho! Did he so? Did he so? Did he so?

When one pot was out, he called for another,
Sing trolly, lolly, lolly, lo!
He kissed the daughter before the mother:
Ho, ho! Did he so? Did he so? Did he so?

And when night came on, to bed they went,
Sing trolly, lolly, lolly, lo!
It was with the mother's own consent:
Ho, ho! Was it so? Was it so? Was it so?

Quoth she: 'What is this, so stiff and warm?'
Sing trolly, lolly, lolly, lo!
' 'Tis Ball, my nag! He will do you no harm!'
Ho, ho! Won't he so? Won't he so? Won't he so?

'But what is this, hangs under his chin?'
Sing trolly, lolly, lolly, lo!
' 'Tis the bag he puts his provender in!'
Ho, ho! Is it so? Is it so? Is it so?

Quoth he: 'What is this?' Quoth she: ' 'Tis a well.'
Sing trolly, lolly, lolly, lo!
'Where Ball, your nag, may drink his fill!'
Ho, ho! May he so? May he so? May he so?

'But what if my nag should chance to slip in?'
Sing trolly, lolly, lolly, lo!
'Then catch hold of the grass that grows on the brim!'
Ho, ho! Must I so? Must I so? Must I so?

'But what if the grass should chance to fail?'
Sing trolly, lolly, lolly, lo!
'Shove him in by the head! Pull him out by the tail!'
Ho, ho,! Must I so? Must I so? Must I so?

The Trooper Watering His Nag is an early example of a recurrent narrative in the songs of fighting men—a soldier who calls at a drinking shop and beds with the landlady's or landlord's daughter. The theme culminated in *A German Officer Crossed the Line* and *Mademoiselle From Armenteers*. It was included in an eighteenth-century anthology of traditional and contemporary popular songs, D'Urfey's *Pills to Purge Melancholy*. Many displayed the robust ribaldry and delight in *double entendre* characteristic of the English in the sixteenth, seventeenth, and early eighteenth centuries.

Twenty Toes

Here's to the game of twenty toes,
It's played all over the town:
The girls play it with ten toes up,
The boys with ten toes down.

Two Toasts

1

Here's to the Tree of Life
That ladies love to scan.
It stands between two stones
Upon the Isle of Man.
Here's to the little bush
That did that tree entwine.
It blossoms once a month
And bears fruit once in nine.

2

Here's to woman, lovely woman,
Who blossoms once a month
And bears fruit once in nine.
She's the only creature
Living this side of hell
Who can draw milk from a coconut
Without breaking the shell.

The Village Blacksmith

Under the spreading chestnut tree
The village smith he sat.
   Amusing himself
   By abusing himself
And catching the load in his hat.

We Are the Boys

We are the boys who fear no noise
When the thundering cannons roar.
We are the heroes of the night,
And we'd sooner f**k than fight,
We're the heroes of the Stand-Back Fusiliers.

We're Here Because

We're here
Because
We're here
Because
We're here
Because
We're here.

We're here
Because
We're here
Because
We're here
Because
We're here.

Sung fatalistically to the poignant air *Auld Lang Syne*. 'Here' was the grim First World War trench.

We've Had No Duff

Air: 'Lead Kindly Light'

We've had no duff,
We've had no duff today,
We've had no duff!
We've had no duff,
No duff at all today,
We've had no duff,
No duff at all today!

We've had no beer,
We've had no beer today,
We've had no beer!
We've had no beer,
No beer at all today,
We've had no beer,
No beer at all today!

We've had no stout,
We've had no stout today,
We've had no stout!
We've had no stout,
No stout at all today,
We've had no stout,
No stout at all today!

We've had no rum,
We've had no rum today,
We've had no rum!
We've had no rum,
No rum at all today,
We've had no rum,
No rum at all today!

We've had no fun,
We've had no fun today,
We've had no fun!
We've had no fun,
No fun at all today,
We've had no fun,
No fun at all today!

We've had no c**t,
We've had no c**t today,
We've had no c**t!
We've had no c**t,
No c**t at all today,
We've had no c**t,
No c**t at all today!

When This Bloody War is Over

Sung to the hymn tune: 'Take It To The Lord In Prayer'.

When the bloody war is over,
Oh, how happy I shall be!
When I get my civvy clothes on,
No more soldiering for me.
No more church parades on Sunday,
No more asking for a pass,
I can tell the Sergeant Major:
'Stick yer passes up yer arse!'

When the bloody war is over,
Oh, how happy I shall be!
When I get my civvy clothes on,
No more soldiering for me.
Then I'll sound my own reveille,
Then I'll make my own tattoo;
No more N.C.O.s to curse me,
No more bleedin' army stew.

The Woodpecker Song

I put my finger in a woodpecker's hole,
And the woodpecker said: 'God bless my soul,
Take it out,
Take it out,
Take it out,
Remove it.'

I removed my finger from the woodpecker's hole,
And the woodpecker said: 'God bless my soul,
Put it back,
Put it back,
Put it back,
Replace it.'

I replaced my finger in the woodpecker's hole,
And the woodpecker said: 'God bless my soul,
Turn it round,
Turn it round,
Turn it round,
Revolve it.'

I revolved my finger in the woodpecker's hole,
And the woodpecker said: 'God bless my soul,
Pull it out,
Pull it out,
Pull it out,
Retract it.'

I retracted my finger from the woodpecker's hole,
And the woodpecker said: 'God bless my soul,
Take a sniff,
Take a sniff,
Take a sniff,
Revolting.'

Yoho

He put his hand upon her toe,
Yoho, yoho.
He put his hand upon her toe,
Yoho, yoho.
He put his hand upon her toe,
She said: 'Soldier, you're mighty slow.
Get in, get out, quit ****ing about,
Yoho, yoho.'

He put his hand upon her calf,
Yoho, yoho.
He put his hand upon her calf,
Yoho, yoho.
He put his hand upon her calf,
She said: 'Soldier, you're there by half.
Get in, get out, quit ****ing about,
Yoho, yoho.'

He put his hand upon her knee,
Yoho, yoho.
He put his hand upon her knee,
Yoho, yoho.
He put his hand upon her knee,
She said: 'Soldier, you're teasing me.
Get in, get out, quit ****ing about,
Yoho, yoho.'

He put his hand above her knee,
Yoho, yoho.
He put his hand above her knee,
Yoho, yoho.
He put his hand above her knee,
She said: 'Soldier, you're pleasing me.
Get in, get out, quit ****ing about,
Yoho, yoho.'

He put his hand high up her thigh,
Yoho, yoho.
He put his hand high up her thigh,
Yoho, yoho.
He put his hand high up her thigh,
She said: 'Soldier, you're mighty sly.
Get in, get out, quit ****ing about,
Yoho, yoho.'

He put his hand upon her tit,
Yoho, yoho.
He put his hand upon her tit,
Yoho, yoho.
He put his hand upon her tit,
She said: 'Soldier, squeeze it a bit.
Get in, get out, quit ****ing about,
Yoho, yoho.'

He put his hand low down her tum,
Yoho, yoho.
He put his hand low down her tum,
Yoho, yoho.
He put his hand low down her tum,
She said: 'Soldier, you'll make me come,
Get in, get out, quit ****ing about,
Yoho, yoho.'

He put his hand upon her rear,
Yoho, yoho.
He put his hand upon her rear,
Yoho, yoho.
He put his hand upon her rear,
She said: 'Soldier, you're getting near.
Get in, get out, quit ****ing about,
Yoho, yoho.'

He put his hand upon her bum,
Yoho, yoho.
He put his hand upon her bum,
Yoho, yoho.
He put his hand upon her bum,
She said: 'Soldier, now that feels rum.
Get in, get out, quit ****ing about,
Yoho, yoho.'

He put his hand upon her thatch,
Yoho, yoho.
He put his hand upon her thatch,
Yoho, yoho.
He put his hand upon her thatch,
She said: 'Soldier, you're starting to scratch.
Get in, get out, quit ****ing about,
Yoho, yoho.'

He put his hand upon her twat,
Yoho, yoho.
He put his hand upon her twat,
Yoho, yoho.
He put his hand upon her twat,
She said: 'Soldier, I fancy that.
Get in, get out, quit ****ing about,
Yoho, yoho.'

He put his pud into her twat,
Yoho, yoho.
He put his pud into her twat,
Yoho, yoho.
He put his pud into her twat,
She said: 'Soldier, what are you at?
Get in, get out, quit ****ing about,
Yoho, yoho.'

And now she works in Aldershot,
Yoho, yoho.
And now she works in Aldershot,
Yoho, yoho.
And now she works in Aldershot,
She says: 'Soldier, let's see what you've
   got!
Get in, get out, quit ****ing about,
Yoho, yoho.'

And now she's in a wooden box,
Yoho, yoho.
And now she's in a wooden box,
Yoho, yoho.
And now she's in a wooden box,
She died from too much soldiery pox.
Get in, get out, quit ****ing about,
Yoho, yoho.'

The Young Harlot of Crete

There was a young harlot of Crete,
Whose ****ng was far, far too fleet.
   So they tied down her ass
   With a length of old brass
To give them a much longer treat.

When the Nazis landed in Crete
This young harlot had to compete
   With so many Storm Troopers
   Who were using their poopers
For betters things than to excrete.

Our subversive young harlot of Crete
Was led to fifth-column deceit.
   When the paratroops landed
   Her trade she expanded
By at once going down on their meat.

Then this lively young harlot of Crete
She decided to be very neat.
   Said she: 'I'm too high class
   For plain common ass,
And I'll wash every prick that I treat.'

But at last this fine harlot of Crete
Was hawking her meat in the street.
   Ambling out one fine day
   In a casual way,
She clapped up the whole British Fleet.

Index of First Lines

A company of Grenadier Guards   130
A fanatic gun-lover named Crust   134
A German officer crossed the line   63
A girl of uncertain nativity   135
A gouty old colonel said: 'Tush!'   137
A man in the battle of Aix   127
A muvver was barfin' 'er biby one night   29
A prisoner in Château d'If   127
A prosperous merchant in Rhône   128
A sunburnt bloody stockman stood   10
A very odd pair are the Pitts   131
An innocent soldier named Stave   133
An old Japanese samurai named Haki   130
Après la guerre finie   9

Dan, Dan the sanitary man   25
Do your balls hang low?   26
Don't dip your wick in a W.A.C.   27
Down in the slums of a Rangoon back street   89

Eff 'em all, eff 'em all   28

Fat old Field-Marshal Goering   136
Frankie and Johnny were lovers   33

He grabbed me round my slender neck   112
He put his hand upon her toe   152
Here's to the game of twenty toes   142
Here's to the good old beer   44
Here's to the Tree of Life   143
Here's to woman, lovely woman   143
Hitler has only got one ball   94

I didn't want to join the army   47
I first met Nellie 'Awkins   93
I lost my arm in the army   49
I put my finger in a woodpecker's hole   150

I wore a tunic   50
I'll eat when I'm hungry   116
In Amsterdam there dwelt a maid   31
In her sweet little Alice-blue gown   53
In the shade of the old apple tree   55
It was Christmas Day in the workhouse   24

John Brown's baby's got a pimple on his—SHUSH!   56

Les cocottes de la ville de Marseille   57
Life presents a dismal picture   58

Meat rationing did not terrify Miss Davey   129
My brother lies over the ocean   15
My name is Captain Hall   17
My Nelly's a whore   92

No bloody sports   95

Oh, give me a home   96
Oh, Mademoiselle from Amiens   85
Oh, Mademoiselle from Armenteers   71, 79
Oh, Mademoiselle from Gay Paree   86
Oh, Mademoiselle from Montparnasse   85
Oh, Mademoiselle from Old Verdun   86
Oh, Mademoiselle from St. Nazaire   85
Oh, Mademoiselle from the town of Grasse   86
Oh, the men they wash the dishes, in Mobile   54
Oh, the peters they are small   101
Oh, this is number one   113
Old King Cole was a bugger for the hole   99

Plump old Colonel Breech-Cantor   136

Raining, raining, raining   110

Said a lusty young soldier named Mickey   135
Said a promiscuous lecherous Nazi   134
She was poor but she was honest   124
Since donning a uniform, Joe   135

The bells of hell go ting-a-ling-a-ling   12
The fortunes of peace   7
The fortunes of war   7
The good ship's name was Venus   39
The old black bull came down from the mountain   97
The orderly sergeant says   100
The prick of a young man of Kew   130
The sergeant-major's having a time   87
The sexual life of the camel   121
The sexual life of the dodo   122
The Squire had a daughter, so fair and so tall   123
There once was a Colonel Defoe   128
There once was a gouty old colonel   128
There was a G.I. name of Snyder   133
There was a young army cadet   127
There was a young harlot of Crete   157
There was a young man from Berlin   132
There was a young man of Jaipur   133
There was a young man, Mussolini   132
There was a young Nazi amoeba   129
There was a young sergeant named Schmidt   134
There was a young soldier, McGill   129
There was an old soldier of Rheims   136
There was an old whore of Marseille   132
There was an old woman who lived under a hill   139
There was Andy, Andy, feeling randy dandy   103
There's a charming young girl in Tobruk   131
This bloody town's a bloody cuss   51
Tiddleywinks, Old Man   138
Under the spreading chestnut tree   144

We 'ad a bleed'n' sparrer wot   13
We are Fred Karno's army   38
We are the boys who fear no noise   145
We're here because we're here   146
We've had no duff   147
When he tried to inject his huge whanger   131
When I was a bachelor I lived by myself   32
When the bloody war is over   149
Wot a marf 'e'd got   30